CHAMPIONS
OF
INVENTION

BY
JOHN HUDSON TINER

Master
Books

First printing: March 2000

Copyright © 1999 by Master Books, Inc. All rights reserved. No part of this book may be used or reproduced in any manner whatsoever without written permission of the publisher, except in the case of brief quotations in articles and reviews. For information write: Master Books, Inc., P.O. Box 727, Green Forest, AR 72638.

ISBN: 0-89051-278-7
Library of Congress Number: 99-67329

Cover by Farewell Communications

Printed in the United States of America

Please visit our website for other great titles:
www.masterbooks.net

For information regarding publicity for author interviews, contact Dianna Fletcher at (870) 438-5288.

This book is dedicated
to
Hite and Glenda Tiner.

CONTENTS

1

BOOKS BY
THE MILLIONS

What is the most important invention of all time? Experts agree that the printing press had the greatest impact on the world. It was invented by John Gutenberg. He was born in Germany about the year 1400. We know little about his early days. He earned a living at various times as a goldsmith and as a stonecutter.

He grew up at a time when people made books by carefully copying them by hand. All books were copied with great care. Those who copied the Bible took special precautions to guard against errors. They proofread a finished page carefully. As an added check, they counted every letter on the page. Each page had to have the same number of letters as the same page in the original document. A person working alone needed about seven years to copy the complete Bible.

People also copied writing by carving a page on a block of wood and printing from it. They carved these wooden blocks exactly like the page, but with writings and drawings reversed. A few hundred sheets could be printed from one block. Ink would then soften the wood and cause blurred, messy pages.

Books were few in number and far too expensive for most people. Only governments, churches, and universities could have large libraries. The owner of a Bible or a dozen other books could be considered a rich person.

Churches would put an open Bible on display. They would turn the page once a week so people could read it.

In 1436, Gutenberg studied how to make mechanical copies of books. He had the idea of using movable type for printing. Each letter would be on the end of a separate bar. A printer could assemble individual letters as a block of type for the page of a book. He could print the page time and again. Then the printer could rearrange the letters to make the next page. A printer could make several hundred identical copies of a book.

Gutenberg worked for years to perfect the process. The metal for the type gave him trouble. Lead flattened under pressure. Iron cracked. Set type inked unevenly. The paper blurred. Unsuccessful experiments took all of his money.

Gutenberg felt certain his idea would work. He needed money desperately. In 1450, he formed a partnership with a business associate. This time he started from the beginning. He realized that printing was a process that involved several steps. A single invention alone would not ensure success. He began fresh and worked on each part until he had it right — the type, printing press, paper, and ink all had to work together.

He began with moveable type. The tiny metal letters had to all be the same size so he could interchange them with one another. They had to lock together evenly as a flat surface. They had to stand up to repeated impressions. He made the type from copper and this time the letters worked perfectly.

The press would push the paper evenly against the block of type. His first machine used parts from a press that squeezed juice from grapes. Instead of flattening grapes, a handle turned a screw to flatten the paper firmly against the block of type. It gave an even impression across the entire sheet of paper.

He experimented with ink. It had to stick to the metal type and then transfer to paper. He developed a new oil-based ink. It was entirely different in chemical composition from ink for wood blocks. He mixed the ink himself.

He even tested paper. Was it the best surface for printing?

The Egyptians had written on papyrus, a rough surface made from reeds. The Chinese had made a paper from bamboo. They also wrote on silk. Europeans wrote important documents on parchment made from the skins of sheep or calves.

Paper had come in use as a writing surface in Europe only a couple of hundred years before Gutenberg's time. Both parchment and paper had a smooth surface that would accept ink. For expensive books, he would use parchment. For less expensive books he would use paper so that ordinary people could own books. Paper was the only part of the printing process that he didn't invent himself. Even so, he sought out and ordered the best paper he could find.

Gutenberg combined his many different inventions and improvements. He now had a method to mass-produce books, all with identical pages.

In 1454, one of the greatest events of world history occurred. Gutenberg began to print the first book made by movable type. Until then, he had experimented with smaller manuscripts such as single sheets, calendars, and religious tracts. He

put six presses in operation. He set type for his most monu-
mental task: printing the entire Bible.

John Gutenberg wanted the printed Bibles to be as beautiful as any handcopied one. He chose attractive type design and
took pains to make each page perfect. His excellent workman-
ship paid off. Gutenberg's Bible was not only the first book
ever printed, but many people consider it the most beautiful
book as well. Seldom does a new invention begin at its greatest
point. His achievement has never been matched.

Each Bible had 1,282 pages, 42 lines on a page, divided
into two columns. He printed 300 copes of each page and bound
them together to make 300 identical Bibles. Of the 300 original
books, only 45 complete copies are still in existence today. Each
is priceless. Today, loose sheets from incomplete Bibles sell
for thousands of dollars. At the time, however, the books
Gutenberg printed were less expensive than those made any
other way.

Until the invention of the printing press, Bibles were rare
and difficult to find. Martin Luther, the German religious leader,
did not see a complete Bible until he was an adult. Soon printers published Bibles on paper in everyday languages such as
German, English, and French. The price dropped so low even
ordinary people could own a Bible. For the first time, common
people had a Bible they could own and read for themselves.
Printing swept Europe. It became a new and successful profes-
sion. Within 50 years more than nine million copies of books
had been printed.

Little is known about Gutenberg himself. Not a single portrait was made of him during his lifetime. Not a single line of his
own handwriting has been uncovered. We do know that
Gutenberg's printing press made it possible for new ideas to spread
with explosive suddenness. Scientists, religious scholars, and
thoughtful citizens could share their ideas easily and quickly.
Gutenberg's invention started several separate revolutions.

Books by the founders of modern science spread the news
about recent discoveries.

On May 24, 1543, Polish astronomer Copernicus published *On the Revolution of the Celestial Sphere*. In that book he gave evidence that the sun and not the earth was at the center of the planetary system. He correctly stated that the earth is a globe that spins on its axis. The earth and all the planets revolve around the sun.

Andreas Vesalius was a Flemish scientist who lived at about the same time as Copernicus. Vesalius studied the human body and taught at a medical school. He discovered that many of the ideas about the construction of the human body were in error. In 1543, he published *The Fabric of the Human Body*. This major work was published in seven volumes. Vesalius detailed his own discoveries and corrected the more than 200 errors he had found in ancient books. It created a revolution in medical studies. These two books, Copernicus' *On the Revolution of the Celestial Sphere* and Vesalius' *The Fabric of the Human Body*, began revolutions not only in astronomy and life science, but in all of science. The two books, which were published the same year, mark the start of the Scientific Revolution.

Vesalius also included 300 illustrations in his book. He chose Jan Stephen van Calcar, a young student of Titian, to refine his sketches so the essential points could be quickly grasped. The drawings showed the human body in natural poses. Printers saw that illustrations helped increase the sale of their books. They began to hire artists to provide illustrations. In addition to illustrating books, the drawings could be sold as single sheets. Even poor people could afford a single drawing. The printing press increased an interest in art that that was part of the Renaissance, or rebirth, in Europe that began in the 1500s.

At the same time, people read the Bible in their own language. Until the time of the printing press, Bibles were written in Latin or Greek, the language of scholars. William Tyndale translated the whole New Testament into English in 1525 and Martin Luther translated the New Testament into German in 1534. This started a spiritual awakening known as the Reformation that swept across Europe.

Printing also made it possible for ordinary citizens to become informed about current events. Before the development of movable metal type, news spread by word of mouth, by written letters, or by single sheets of paper posted on walls or doors. The first newspapers were printed starting early in the 1600s. People read the news and demanded a greater role in governing their day-to-day lives. This caused governments to be more democratic. It led to the American Revolution, the Declaration of Independence, the Constitution, and the Bill of Rights.

Before the invention of the printing press, new ideas had to be circulated by handwritten manuscripts. Those in power did not encourage original thought because new ideas led to unrest. Dictators could hunt down and destroy a few handwritten manuscripts. It was far more difficult to silence new ideas once they were expressed in hundreds or thousands of books.

Do you judge the success of an invention by the number of people it has affected? If the answer is yes, then Gutenberg was the most successful inventor of all time.

Why did Gutenberg succeed when many others tried the same task and failed? What did Gutenberg think about his success?

As his life drew to a close, Gutenberg stated the reason for his success. In a large dictionary published in 1460, he explained that his work had been under "the protection of the All-Highest, Who often reveals to the humble what He conceals from the wise."

2

THE POWER OF STEAM

P eople in the ancient world had few choices for getting work done. They could use wind or water or muscles. Sailing ships caught the wind to carry them along. On shore, windmills were used to turn stones to grind grain. Water from rushing streams or behind dams could be used to turn mill wheels and grind grain. Wind was unreliable, and fast-flowing water was often unavailable in the location where it was needed. Muscle power was the only other choice. The muscles of horses carried riders and pulled chariots. Oxen pulled plows and heavily laden wagons.

Often, human beings had to do heavy work with their own muscles. The Egyptians built the pyramids with the help of as many as 100,000 slaves. In Exodus, the Bible describes how the Hebrews were slaves to the pharaoh until Moses brought the message for Pharaoh to let God's people go. Roman ships and later those of the Vikings had sails, but they also depended on the straining efforts of the crew pulling on oars when the wind failed. In the American Colonies, farmers in the north had large families so the children could help with the chores and work a larger farm. In the south, cotton farmers kept slaves to do the manual labor.

The invention of the steam engine changed the world. It reduced the oppressive use of manual labor and provided reliable power in places where water and wind were not practical.

Although many people had a hand in making steam power possible, the one individual who made it practical was Scottish inventor James Watt.

Because of poor health, James Watt stayed at home as a child. His mother taught him to read and write. The family was prosperous during his early days. As he grew older, however, his father's fortunes reversed. By the time James left home, he had to take a job as the apprentice to an instrument maker.

He studied in England and then returned to Scotland. The city of Glasgow refused to issue a permit for him to open his repair shop. They believed he needed more experience. He took a job repairing instruments for the University of Glasgow. Having to work at the university was a fortunate event. James Watt now repaired instruments for scientists. He became a friend with Joseph Black, a chemist. Joseph Black knew a lot about steam power.

The idea of putting steam to work goes back at least two thousand years. Hero of Alexander made a metal sphere with two nozzles on opposite sides of the sphere. Steam from boiling water in the sphere escaped through the nozzles. This caused the sphere to spin. The effect is similar to the action of the water that causes a lawn sprinkler to whirl.

In the late 1600s, Thomas Newcomen had developed a crude and inefficient steam engine. Newcomen based his engine on a simple observation. Partially fill a bottle with boiling water. Close the bottle with a stopper. As the water condenses, the stopper pops into the bottle. Outside air pushes the stopper into the partial vacuum in the bottle.

Newcomen's engine worked by filling a metal cylinder with hot steam. Cold water cooled the metal cylinder. The steam condensed back to water. It caused a partial vacuum, pulling in a piston. The piston pulled on a lever to operate the pump. Mine owners used the engines to pump water out of flooded coal mines. The Newcomen machine was both clumsy and inefficient. Only a few of his engines were built.

The university had a model of the Newcomen engine. They

gave it to James Watt to repair. He used the opportunity learn all he could about steam power. He talked with Joseph Black. Their calculations showed that Newcomen's engine wasted most of the energy from the steam.

The problem was the chamber. It had to be first heated and then cooled. Hot steam entered the chamber. The cold water chilled the cylinder.

James Watt didn't want to merely repair the engine. He set out to improve it. He added a second chamber to receive the steam. The condenser chamber could be kept cold. The first chamber, the cylinder, could be kept hot. Now both cylinders moved the piston. Hot steam entered the cylinder and pushed on the piston from one side. The change of steam to water in the condenser pulled on it from the other side.

Watt's change made all the difference. The engine worked much more efficiently. It ran more quickly. Two cylinders avoided the delay of waiting for a single cylinder to change temperature from cold to hot as in Newcomen's engine.

James Watt's change impressed Joseph Black. He gave James a loan of money. He urged the young inventor to continue improving the steam engine. James did make many improvements. He insulated the steam cylinder. He added a pressure gauge. He also attached a flywheel. The heavy flywheel served to store energy. The steam engine ran more smoothly. Giving motion to the spinning flywheel evened out the sudden surge of power each time the piston moved.

James Watt took out the first patent on an improved steam engine in 1769. He continued to make improvements. By 1775 he was ready to build steam engines and sell them. Watt himself did not have a good head for business. He was smart enough to see this shortcoming in himself. He formed a partnership with Matthew Boulton. Mr. Boulton was a talented business-man. He had money to invest. Together they went into the steam engine business.

Until then, the main source of power had been muscle power — either human muscles or animal muscles. Mills and

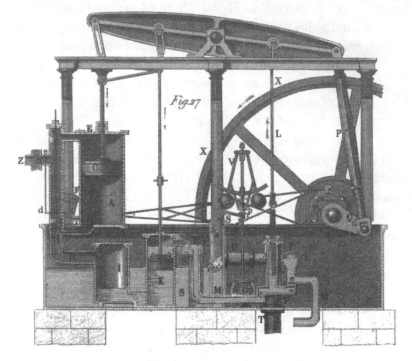

Watt's steam engine

factories sometimes used windmills and waterwheels, but these sources of energy needed dependable winds or a constant supply of running water. These problems severely limited the productive capacity of industry. Watt's engines replaced the toil of humans and horses. He could locate his engine anywhere.

As a selling point, James Watt compared the power of his engine with that of a horse. He tested a strong horse. The horse pulled a rope that went over a pulley to a heavy weight. The horse could raise 150 pounds a height of four feet in one second. Watt called this a horsepower. A seven horsepower engine could do the work of seven horses.

Engineers still use the horsepower to measure power. In the metric system the unit of power is the watt, named in honor of James Watt. One horsepower is 746 watts. A human being working hard can generate about 1/4 of a horsepower in short bursts.

James Watt also invented a governor to control the speed of the engine. Watt's governor was a spinning rod with two weights. The two weights were hooked to a valve that controlled the flow of steam. If the steam engine gained too much speed, the rod spun faster. The weights swung out. They closed a valve and reduced the flow of steam. The engine ran more slowly. If the steam engine lost too much speed, the weights came back down. This opened the valve. The engines ran more quickly.

Until then, a human operator opened and closed a valve to keep the engine running at a set speed. Watt used a little mechanical device to do the work previously done by a person. If the governor had been Watt's only invention, he would have been famous. It was the first automatic control of machinery.

His steam engines sold briskly. James Watt retired from the steam engine business in 1800. Other inventors put steam engines to new uses. In 1807, American inventor and engineer Robert Fulton (1765–1815) ordered a steam engine from Watt's factory. Fulton put the steam engine aboard the riverboat Clermont and fitted it to a paddle wheel. The steam-propelled Clermont made a spectacular run of 150 miles up the Hudson River. Traveling at 4.7 miles per hour, it steamed from New York City to Albany in 32 hours. Sailing vessels normally took four days for the trip. Fulton's steam engine proved popular when used on a passenger boat between New York and Albany, the capitol of New York state. The Clermont was the first efficient steamboat.

The first railroad locomotive was made in 1804 in England. It used a steam engine for power. In 1829, British engineer George Stephenson (1781–1848) built an improved version. His steam locomotive, the Rocket, pulled a load three times its own weight. On one test run it hauled a coach filled with passengers at the incredible speed of 24 miles per hour.

The steamboat and locomotive revolutionized both land

and water transportation. James Watt and his partner earned a good profit.

Gutenberg's invention of the printing press helped start the Scientific Revolution. James Watt's invention of the steam engine helped start the Industrial Revolution. Factories became common. Manufactured goods became much less expensive. Farmers could work larger farms with fewer people. Steam engines could do the work of slaves, and within 100 years of Watt's invention, most countries of the world outlawed slavery. The world's population shifted from rural areas to cities. James Watt's invention changed the world in a fundamental way.

3

A SHOCKING SUBJECT

S uppose a person who lived in ancient Rome two thousand years ago was suddenly transported forward 1,750 years. Suppose he or she walked the streets of Philadelphia in the year 1750. He would see a bustling city that at first glance appeared far different from the ancient Roman city he had left behind. However, by asking questions and examining what they saw, it would not take him long to understand his new location.

Horses still pulled wagons, ships still sailed the ocean, and the flame of fireplaces cooked food. Clocks kept better time than the sundials used in ancient Rome, but the mechanical operation of a clock would be understandable to an ancient engineer. A person with ordinary intelligence could grasp it all. It would be a different world, but one based on ideas known to the ancient Romans. Even a form of the steam engine had been built by the Roman engineer Hero about A.D. 40.

Now move the person forward by 250 years from 1750 to 2000. Now the world has inventions that are far beyond anything known in the ancient world. The ancient visitor would marvel at telephones, televisions, computers, automobiles, airplanes, air-conditioned buildings, and microwave ovens. If he opened the back of a television, he would see wires and circuit boards rather than gears and mechanical linkages. The modern gadgets would appear almost magical rather than scientific.

What made the difference? Electricity. Most of the modern world's most important inventions make use of electric current. Benjamin Franklin was the first scientist to make real progress in understanding and using electricity.

Many people try their hands at a variety of fields before they find a successful occupation. Benjamin Franklin pursued various professions, and he mastered all of them. He made a mark in business, science, literature, politics, and as an inventor.

Benjamin Franklin was born in Boston in 1706 when the American Colonies still answered to Britain. He was the youngest son of 13 children in a Puritan family. He received only two years of formal education. The rest of his education came from his own determination. He read incessantly. He enjoyed books such as John Bunyon's *Pilgrim's Progress*, Plutarch's *Lives*, and Daniel Defoe's *Robinson Crusoe*.

As a teenager, Ben worked in a print shop owned by his brother. In 1723, Ben left Boston and journeyed to Philadelphia. He arrived penniless and unknown.

A store owner hired him to go to London to buy goods for sale in America. Only after Ben crossed the Atlantic Ocean did he learn that the businessman was dishonest. He was stranded in London without a return fare. He made the best of the situation by studying printing.

Ben also demonstrated a skill few other people then possessed — the ability to swim. The astonishing sight of him in the water caused people to gather on the banks to watch. A wealthy man was sending his two young sons on a long sea voyage. He hired Ben to teach his boys to swim. Had Benjamin stayed in London longer, it is possible he would have become a full-time swim instructor.

A friend offered to introduce Benjamin Franklin to Isaac Newton, the most famous scientist in the world. Isaac Newton was 83 years old. Before the meeting could take place, Benjamin unexpectedly found passage back to America. He'd lived in England for 18 months.

Once he returned to Philadelphia, Ben opened his own print shop. It prospered. He married. He started a newspaper. He began to print *Poor Richard's Almanack*. Franklin demonstrated another of many talents: writing.

The chief contributor to *Poor Richard's Almanack* was Ben Franklin himself. He had an unusual ability to express difficult ideas in pithy sayings. "A penny saved is a penny earned," he wrote. And, "A man is no taller than when he is on his knees [to pray]." One of his most quoted saying is, "Early to bed, early to rise, makes a man healthy, wealthy, and wise." He took this saying to heart. He would get up at four o'clock to begin the day with prayers.

Later, he wrote a book about his life. It is one of the most famous autobiographies ever written. It is still being published and read after all of these years. In the first chapter of the book, he declared his thanks to God for blessing him so abundantly.

At age 22, Ben organized a group of young city leaders. They believed their businesses would prosper if the city of Philadelphia were a better place to live. He and his group created a public library, a fire company, a college, and a hospital. They organized a night watch to make the streets safer. Philadelphia became the largest city in North America.

In 1748 Ben decided to retire from business and devote himself to other matters. He wanted to perfect some of his inventions, such as a better stove.

Most homes had fireplaces for both cooking and heating. Yet, a fireplace was particularly poor at heating. About four-fifths of the heat escaped up the chimney. The fire needed to be more in the middle of the room. He made a cast iron stove and connected it to the chimney by stovepipes. He didn't patent the invention so people would put it more quickly into use. Although he called the invention the Philadelphia stove, it became known as the Franklin stove. Soon, Franklin's stove was a common fixture in both the Colonies in America and in Europe.

By 1750 he'd become well known as a civil leader, writer,

and inventor. What could he turn to next? He decided to study static electricity. Franklin had experienced static electricity. He rubbed his feet across the fur of a bear skin rug on a cold, dry day, and then touched a metal doorknob. With a sudden crackle an electric spark jumped from his hand to the doorknob. For some people who were especially sensitive to electricity it could be an uncomfortable experience. Rubbing a comb briskly through clean, dry hair gave the comb a static charge. It would attract small pieces of paper.

Franklin read about electricity. He found that the first scientist to report about static electricity lived more than 600 years before Christ. Thales of Melitus, a Greek scientist, noticed that when he stroked amber with wool the amber would pick up feathers or straw. Amber is a hard fossil resin that forms naturally from tree sap. This semitransparent mineral has a beautiful yellow color. It is sometimes used for jewelry. Electricity and electron are from *elektron*, the Greek word for amber.

In the 1500s, William Gilbert, an English physician, showed that substances other than amber can have an electric charge. He found that glass, hard rubber, rock crystals such as quartz, and gemstones such as diamond and sapphire would take a charge when rubbed with wool, fur, or silk.

Franklin learned that friction causes static electricity. Rubbing a rubber rod with fur gave it a static electric charge. The charged rod would pick up small bits of paper or lint. He brought charged bodies near one another. Sometimes they repelled each other. Other times they attracted each other. These confusing and contradictory observations puzzled scientists.

Franklin simplified matters by supposing the existence of a single electric fluid. If a body had too much of the fluid, it would have an excess charge. If it had too little of the fluid, it would have a deficit charge. He used the signs plus, +, and minus, -, to show the difference. In the Middle Ages, merchants weighed the product they sold. If a crate was under weight they marked it with a bar, -, to show it was below the right amount. Later, they added more of the product to bring the package up to weight or even a little over. They put a vertical mark through the bar, +, to show its weight had been corrected. Franklin introduced identified the glass rod rubbed with silk as having a positive, +, or excess amount of the fluid. He identified the rubber rod stroked with wool as having a negative, -, or deficit amount of electric fluid.

Scientists later learned the electric fluid is electrons, one of the three building blocks that make up all matter. Electrons have a negative electric charge. Electrons flow easily. Friction of two bodies rubbing together is enough to cause the transfer. A body that gains electrons has a negative charge. A body that loses electrons has a positive charge.

Franklin discovered three laws about static electricity. He rubbed a glass rod with silk, which gave it a positive charge. When he brought it near another glass rod with a positive charge, the two glass rods pushed one another away even before they touched. Two glass rods, each with a positive charge, repelled one another. He rubbed a rubber rod with fur, which gave it a negative charge. When he brought it near another rubber rod with a negative charge, the two rubber rods pushed one another away. They, too, repelled one another. This demonstrated Franklin's first law of static electricity: like static electric charges repel.

He brought a rubber rod with a negative charge near a glass rod with a positive charge. They attracted one another. This is the second law: unlike static electric charges attract.

He also found that uncharged bodies are attracted to charged bodies. A positively charged glass rod will pick up uncharged bits of paper or lint, and so will a negatively charged rubber rod. This is the third law: bodies charged with static electricity will attract uncharged ones.

For his electrical experiments, a friend sent Benjamin a Leyden jar. A scientist who taught physics at the University of Leyden in Holland invented it. It could store a static electric charge for a short period. It was a glass jar with a metal foil on the inside and outside. The glass of the jar separated the foil.

The lid was an insulating cork stopper. In the center of the cork stopper was a metal knob on a rod. Electricity enters and leaves the jar through the metal knob. Franklin generated static electricity by turning a glass globe that rubbed against felt. Felt is a pad made of animal fur. He collected a strong static charge by putting the knob of the Leyden jar against the glass globe.

Franklin showed the power of electricity by preparing his Christmas turkey. He killed the bird instantly with a powerful shock from a fully charged Leyden jar. Then to roast the turkey, he used an electric spark to ignite wood in his fireplace.

Franklin carried out one of the most spectacular and dangerous experiments ever conducted in science. In 1752 he flew a kite during a lightning storm. He realized the danger and took precautions. He stood under a porch with a metal roof and held the string of the kite by a dry silk ribbon. The lightning struck a metal rod he had put on the kite. Lightning came down the wet string to a key. He brought the key to the knob of a Leyden jar sitting on a table. He captured some of the lightning.

In the laboratory, Franklin compared the captured lightning to static electricity. He ran the stored lightning through the same tests as static electricity. He got identical results. Lightning was a powerful discharge of static electricity but on a much grander scale. The crackle of a static spark and the roar of thunder were both caused by electricity zapping through air.

Franklin's difficult kite experiment was dangerous. Two years later a scientist tried to capture some lightning and died in the attempt.

Many buildings in Franklin's time were made of wood. Lightning strikes often set fire to these buildings. Most cities had woefully inadequate fire companies to fight the blaze. For that reason, lightning storms were frightening events. For farmers with barns filled with hay, grain, and farm animals, a lightning strike could destroy their livelihood.

Franklin's understanding of electricity made it possible for him to invent lightning rods. Placing lightning rods along

roof ridges and chimneys greatly reduced the possibility of a lighting strike. These metal conductors had a wire running down to the ground. The rod and ground wire drained away the electric charge before it became strong enough to become a lightning bolt. Even if the building were struck by a bolt of lightning, the wire conducted the lighting harmlessly to the ground

Buildings in America and Europe began to sprout Franklin's lightning rods. He had become world famous. He was the first scientist of note from the American Colonies.

In 1751, the next stage of his life began. Voters elected Benjamin Franklin to the Pennsylvania Assembly. As the years passed, he gained a reputation as an honest and fair politician. He became a champion of self-government. He believed ordinary people should have a role in the political affairs that touched upon their lives.

British rule was growing more oppressive in the Colonies.

It became clear that the only relief would be through independence from England. In 1776 Franklin helped draft the Declaration of Independence. He signed the document. It was a dangerous step. He could be tried for treason and put in prison or even hanged.

Benjamin Franklin sailed to France to enlist their support during the Revolutionary War. He was 80 years old, but as active as ever. He preferred peace to conflict. He represented the new United States at secret peace talks with England.

With the war over, he returned to the States. He triumphed in helping get the Constitution written and supporting George Washington as the first president. He took up two causes that were especially important to him. He worked for better treatment of the American Indians and he also was an active member of a group that opposed slavery.

Religion played a daily role in his life. He says in his autobiography, "There is one God, who made all things. He governs the world by His providence. He ought to be worshiped by adoration, prayer, and thanksgiving. The most acceptable service of God is doing good to men. The soul is immortal. God will certainly reward virtue and punish vice, either here or hereafter."

As an inventor, Benjamin Franklin made the first bifocal reading glasses, the improved Franklin stove, and lightning rods. As a scientist he proposed the use of positive, +, and negative, -, to identify electric charge, stated the three laws of static electricity, and proved that lightning is a form of electricity.

Benjamin Franklin had a major role in developing the ideas on which the United States was based. For that reason, when asked what was Franklin's greatest invention, many people reply, "The United States."

4

LIGHTNING
LINE DOCTOR

F ollowing Benjamin Franklin's study of electricity and
development of lightning rods, almost 50 years passed
before any new electrical inventions were made. The
lack of a dependable supply of electricity hindered scientists
and experimenters. The only way to make electricity was by
friction, the rubbing of two surfaces together. Generating electricity by friction used large clumsy machines that were turned
by a crank.

In 1800 an Italian physicist, Alessandro Volta, found that
two different metals separated by saltwater produced electricity. He built the first batteries. Until then, scientists thought of
electricity as static. Static means having no motion. Volta's
chemical batteries produced a continuous supply of electricity
and this shifted interest in electricity from static electricity to
current electricity.

One of the first inventions that used electric current was
the telegraph invented by Samuel F.B. Morse. As a young person, he set out to be an artist. In 1812 he sailed to England to
study at the Royal Academy. Once in London, Samuel wrote to
his parents telling them of his safe arrival. The fastest mail ship
took a month to cross the Atlantic.

Four weeks would past before his parents could read his

letter. "I only wish," he wrote, "you had this letter now. But three thousand miles are not passed over in an instant."

After two years in England, Samuel Morse returned to the United States. As the years passed, he became the best known and most successful artist in the United States. He developed a style of painting known as "democratic art." He believed that art should elevate a person and portray ideas that would make a person a better citizen. He visited Washington D.C., where he painted the lawmakers at work.

He was a devout Christian who took a leading role in starting Sunday schools. He began a Sunday school in his hometown of New Haven, Connecticut. It was one of the first in the United States. Samuel served as the superintendent. As his portrait business took him all along the eastern seaboard from South Carolina to Massachusetts, he promoted the idea of Sunday schools. He always gave generously to support religious efforts.

At the height of his fame a tragedy struck. He was in Washington, D.C., painting the portraits of famous Americans. Back home his young and beautiful wife unexpectedly became sick and died. The letter telling of her death took eight days getting to him. It arrived too late for him to attend her funeral. It was a terrible blow because they were deeply in love.

Morse moved to New York City. He believed that the completion of the Erie Canal would make New York, and not Philadelphia, the most important city in America. Shipping could proceed from New York City up the Hudson River to Albany and then along the Erie Canal to Lake Erie, one of the Great Lakes.

To overcome his grief at the loss of his wife, Samuel Morse began a free school for art students too poor to attend the expensive schools in New York. He began the National Academy of Design and served as its first president.

After 20 years in America, Samuel returned to Europe as a master painter. He visited all of the great museums and continued to improve his skill as an artist. He studied paintings at the Louvre in Paris, France. There he met Alexander von Humboldt, a German naturalist, explorer, and amateur artist.

In 1799, Alexander von Humboldt had used his own money to make a scientific expedition to South America. He and a companion covered more than 6,000 miles. They paddled down uncharted rivers and hiked through steamy rain forests. They collected plant specimens, charted unexplored territory, and measured temperature, pressure, and magnetic intensity. Von Humboldt showed enormous physical endurance by climbing to 19,280 feet in the Andes. He held the record for the highest mountain climb for 30 years.

Upon his return to Europe, von Humboldt settled in Paris. Over the next 25 years, he wrote more than 30 books about his travels. He had the unusual ability of recognizing talent and encouraging people. When he saw deserving young students, he gave them money to continue their education. About five years before he met Samuel Morse, he had given away all of his money. He returned to Berlin, Germany, where he earned a living as a tutor and by giving public lectures. He visited Paris once a year, and it was on one of those trips that he met Samuel F.B. Morse at the Louvre.

He recognized in the portrait painter a side no one else had noticed. Rather than talking about art, Morse and von Humboldt talked about rapid communication. The French sent messages from mountaintop to mountaintop by towers with sig nal arms that moved up and down. The signal system, known as semaphore, did not work well. On foggy days, the arms were hidden in mist. In The United States, where the distances were greater, it would be nearly useless.

Their discussions turned to lightning and electricity.

"Nothing is faster than lightning," von Humboldt said.

"But electricity is a scientific curiosity," Morse said. "No one has found a way to use it." Baron von Humboldt encouraged Morse to think about a way to use electricity to send messages.

In 1832, Samuel sailed back to America. He had heard of a new invention, an electromagnet. When electricity flowed, the magnet attracted an iron object such as a nail. When the circuit was broken and the electricity ceased, the magnet dropped the nail it had attracted. While aboard the ship, he began thinking about sending messages by electricity. The idea captured his imagination. Could he flash signals instantly anywhere along a wire?

Feverishly, Samuel sketched his basic design. In his invention, electricity flowed through a circuit of wire. It caused an electromagnet to raise and lower a metal lever. A pencil attached to the lever marked dots and dashes on a moving strip of paper.

He called his invention a telegraph. The word means writing at a distance. Samuel Morse devised a code of dots and dashes that stood for letters of the alphabet. The dots and dashes became known as the Morse code.

Samuel gave up all thoughts of art. Instead, he devoted his full time and life savings to building a working model. Within a few months after landing in New York, Samuel showed a crude form of the telegraph to several businessmen.

From the first, Samuel Morse's telegraph worked, but it didn't impress the businessmen. One person said, "It is useful only for the lady of the house to send for the maid in the cellar!"

Samuel struggled to interest people in the telegraph. He said, "We need a fast form of communication. Because of the lack of speedy communication, England and the United States blundered into the War of 1812. They fought a bloody battle in New Or-

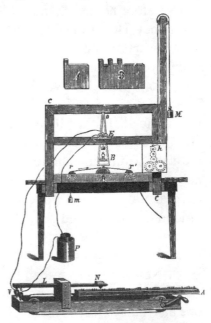

Here is a sketch of Samuel Morse's first electric telegraph. It sent out messages in a series of dots and dashes, called Morse code.

leans 11 days after signing a peace treaty. Because of the lack of quick and dependable communication, my wife died and was buried before I even learned that she'd become ill."

Yet, most people looked upon the telegraph as a plaything of science without any real worth. He traveled to Europe to sell the invention. There he found competing designs. Although his telegraph was vastly superior, England and France did not want to grant patents without giving their citizens the first opportunity to build telegraph lines.

While in France, Samuel Morse attended the announcement of a new invention, the process known as photography. Louis Daguerre had found a way to make a mirror with a memory. Daguerre exposed silver-coated sheets of metal to an image produced by a lens. Then he heated the metal plate in a cabinet containing mercury fumes. The result was a beautiful and permanent record of the image on the silver mirror.

Samuel Morse left France just as Daguerre made the process public. When Morse returned to the United States he built his own equipment. He became one of the first to take photographs in America. He taught the process to students. One of his students was Mathew Brady who would become a famous photographer of the Civil War.

Samuel Morse noticed that the French government gave Louis Daguerre a yearly income for his invention. In turn, Daguerre released it for the whole world to use. Other countries such as Britain often helped people make important inventions, either by a direct payment or by giving them an annual salary so they could continue their work. The United States all but ignored Samuel Morse's efforts. However, his faith in God did not waver. "I am perfectly satisfied that, mysterious as it may seem to me, it has all been ordered in view of my Heavenly Father's guiding hand."

Finally, after 12 years of trying, Samuel convinced the United States government to pay for a test line. He would run it between Baltimore and Washington, D.C. Samuel set the date for the official demonstration of the telegraph: Friday, May 24,

1844. He'd send a message from Washington to Baltimore and back again. Members of Congress came to see the invention. Samuel told them, "At my invitation, Miss Annie G. Ellsworth, the daughter of the Commissioner of Patents, has selected the first official message."

Anne handed him the slip of paper. The message read, "What hath God wrought!" He, of course, recognized it as a quotation from Numbers 23:23 in the Bible. Calmly he tapped out the message. The electric current raced to Baltimore. His assistant echoed it back. The message returned instantly.

"It is an astonishing invention," a senator said.

A newspaper reporter wrote about the amazing telegraph. "In a race between the telegraph line and the railroad line, Mr. Morse's lighting line won."

The telegraph was the first practical use of electricity. Families could quickly learn of the safe arrival of loved ones at faraway destinations. Railroads could report track conditions and prevent accidents. For the first time, a communication network rapidly collected weather information. Weather forecasts became much more reliable.

The telegraph began to earn a profit. During all of the difficult years of trying, Samuel had lived in near poverty. Once, he grew so weak from lack of food that he nearly fainted. Despite these hardships, Samuel gave the first money from his invention to a church in Washington so the congregation could begin a Sunday school.

The telegraph became one of the top ten inventions of all time. Its invention assured Samuel Morse's place in history.

Honors showered upon him. Yale conferred upon him an honorary L.L.D. degree. The letters stood for Latin words meaning doctor of letters. Playfully, Samuel always insisted that L.L.D. stood for "Lightning Line Doctor."

What did Samuel Morse think of his invention? "I agree with that sentence of Annie Ellsworth, 'What hath God wrought!' It is His work. 'Not unto us, but to Thy name, O Lord, be all the praise.' "

5

GENIUS IN
A BOOKSTORE

I magine a world without television, computers, video games — or even toasters or electric doorbells. Such a world existed only two hundred years ago. One of the inventors who was responsible for bringing electricity into everyday use was Michael Faraday.

Michael Faraday had been born in a small town in England. His father was a blacksmith and his mother a farmer's daughter. Shortly after he was born his father looked for a better-paying job and moved to London. They took lodging in rooms over a coach house. Faraday had nine brothers and sisters.

London of the early 1800s had no free schools. Instead, parents paid tutors to train their children. Michael's family was desperately poor. Because of the expense, they could keep him in school for only a few months. He learned to read, write, and do simple arithmetic. His parents taught him at home as best they could, including their strong Christian principles. God would attend to his well-being, they explained. If he wished more in his life, then he could follow the biblical instruction to "Ask, seek and knock" (Matt. 7:7). Michael Faraday tried to remain faithful to God throughout his life.

The children of poor families were expected to work. By

Michael Faraday

the time he was 13 years old, Michael had to find a way to help support his family. His father did not think he was strong enough to be a blacksmith or do heavy work in factories. Children with a slight build such as Michael's often became chimney sweeps. They cleaned the chimneys that connected fireplaces in the several floors of a large building. They were lowered into the chimney by their ankles and crawled through the brick passageways. It was dirty, dangerous work. The soot and ash caused lung ailments.

Michael Faraday was fortunate, then, to receive an apprenticeship with a bookbinder, Mr. George Riebau. The man had no children and treated Faraday as if he were his own son. Mr. Riebau encouraged Michael to read the books that came through the shop. In this way, Michael gained a better education. He also became skilled at drawing from instruction given by a French painter who lodged with Mr. Riebau. The artist loaned him books and taught him sketching. Michael used the books of the shop as his texts and guides. He taught himself to speak and to write correctly. Through self-study, he gained a better education.

Michael was fascinated with science. He began repeating experiments described in the books. He wanted to attend the science lectures of the great English chemist Humphry Davy, professor at the Royal Institution of London. Davy was

England's best known and most successful scientist. At his lectures, Davy showed the most recent scientific inventions. Gases exploded. Bolts of electricity jumped between wires. People flocked to the lectures. However, costs of tickets to the lectures were far more than Michael could afford.

One of the customers of the shop, Mr. Dance, had some tickets to Davy's science lectures. He gave the tickets to Michael Faraday. Michael attended the lectures and took careful notes. Afterward, he took the notes and made colored drawings to accompany them. He beautifully bound the notes and illustrations in a leather book and presented them to Humphry Davy by way of introduction. Michael begged to work as Davy's assistant.

The notebook impressed the great scientist. However, he had no openings at the Royal Institution but he promised to keep Michael Faraday in mind. Davy had a habit of tasting and sniffing chemicals. He was not as careful as he should have been around chemicals. Shortly after Michael Faraday sent the book, an explosion of nitrogen chloride blinded Davy. He continued to work and hired Michael for a few weeks to read to him and write his correspondence. When his vision recovered, he let Michael go. "I am sorry," Davy said. "There still is no opening on my staff."

The next morning Davy sent for Michael. During the night, one of his assistants had been involved in a fight. The assistant was dismissed from the Royal Institution for brawling. Davy offered a job to Michael Faraday. He warned, "Science is a harsh mistress and poorly rewarding. You'll make far more money in the bookstore."

Michael Faraday accepted the offer. He was the lowest assistant, hardly more than a bottle washer. It did pay less than his salary at the bookshop. For Michael Faraday, it was his big break. "I count it worth something to be working beside one of England's great scientists," Michael Faraday explained.

Only seven months after starting at the Royal Institution, Michael Faraday became Davy's personal assistant. Davy took him on a grand tour of Europe. They met many of the leading scientists in France, Italy, and other countries. Michael Faraday soaked up all the knowledge he could. Until that trip, he had never traveled more than 12 miles from London.

The unschooled son of a blacksmith now served as assistant to the best-known scientist in the world. Incredible! Was it luck? Michael Faraday didn't think so. He knew that good things come to those who served the Lord. He'd succeeded through hard work and trust in God.

Michael Faraday served as Davy's assistant for seven years. He became director of the laboratory. In 1821, Faraday married Sarah Barnard. He preferred to stay close to his laboratory, so they lived in an attic apartment above the Royal Institution.

Michael Faraday experimented with electricity. He read about a discovery by Hans Christian Orested, a Danish scientist. Orested had shown that electricity running through a wire pulls a compass needle off course. A compass needle is a small magnet. Orested concluded that electric current causes a magnetic field around the wire. The wire then either attracts or repels a magnet depending on the direction the current flows.

Michael Faraday took Orested's discovery and expanded on it. Michael built a device in which a wire rotated around a magnet while current flowed in the wire. He proved that that electricity could be changed to mechanical motion. He had made the first electric motor.

Michael Faraday now asked the next question. Could he make electricity by using a magnet? The answer to that question interested scientists. They desperately needed an easy and dependable way to generate electricity. They could make electricity only with clumsy static generators or with crude and expensive chemical batteries.

Michael worked on the problem off and on for several years. It is difficult today to understand all the problems he faced. For instance, he had to insulate copper wire himself. He wrapped wire with strips of cloth torn from one of his wife's old aprons.

Ten years passed. Michael kept coming back to the problem. Success came on August 29, 1831. Michael thrust a bar magnet through a loop of wire. A small electric current flowed. Then it died. He pulled the magnet out of the loop. Again current flowed, this time in the opposite direction.

The key was motion! In Orested's original experiment, moving electrons in a wire upset a compass needle. In the same way, a moving magnetic field puts electrons in motion. This causes an electric current.

Michael Faraday spun a copper disk between the poles of powerful magnets. He touched the disk at the center and at the edge with copper brushes attached to a wire. As he spun the copper disk, he drew away a continuous supply of electricity. Michael Faraday had invented the first electric generator. He turned the crank and produced a continuous current of electricity.

While building electric motors and electric generators, Michael Faraday also made the first transformers. Transformers step-up or step-down the voltage of a current. Electricity is most efficiently sent cross-country at high voltage. It is most safely used at low voltage. Step-up transformers increase the voltage for electricity going from power stations to cities. Then step-down transformers reduce the voltage to safer levels for home use.

Michael Faraday had only limited mathematical education. He used visual pictures rather than mathematical equations to express his ideas. He introduced the ideas of lines of force and electric and magnetic fields. Around a magnet is a magnetic field. This field can be made visible by sprinkling iron filings on a sheet of paper over the magnet.

The ideas of lines of force and energy fields are key ideas in modern science. Both James Clerk Maxwell and Albert Einstein based much of their work on the idea of fields. Both men were exceptionally good at mathematics. They held Michael Faraday in high regard. Albert Einstein kept a portrait of Michael Faraday on the wall behind his desk.

"I do not feel that I possess anything extraordinary,"

Michael Faraday told a newspaper reporter. "If I do have special talent, it must certainly be perseverance."

Michael Faraday strove to live a humble life. He worked at a minimum wage as director of the Royal Institution. Once, a visitor from the Royal Mint came into the Royal Institution. He found an elderly worker cleaning a table filled with test tubes. The employee walked with a shuffle. His shoulders were bent and he had a full head of white hair. His clothes were well worn. He's the janitor, the visitor decided.

The visitor asked, "Have you worked here long?"

"Almost 50 years," the elderly man replied.

The visitor asked, "Are you well paid?"

"It could be a little better," the old man replied.

The visitor explained, "Maybe I can have a word with the director on your behalf. What is your name?"

"Michael Faraday," was the prompt reply.

Faraday's inventions made him famous. He could have made a fortune from them. However, he and his beloved wife, Sarah, were devout members of a congregation that encouraged its members to live modestly and not accumulate wealth. He gave away much of what he earned. Faraday turned down a knighthood and an offer to become president of the Royal Society. He and his wife lived in an attic apartment above the Royal Institution until the steps became too difficult for Sarah to climb. Queen Victoria gave Faraday and his wife a small home near the Royal Institution. She modified the building to eliminate steps.

Michael Faraday's fame exceeded that of any living scientist. Like Humphry Davy, he began a series of lectures on science. Michael Faraday never forgot his humble beginning. During Christmas, he offered free lectures for children. One of these, about candles, became a favorite of the crowd. He wrote the book *The Chemical History of the Candle* based on his candle lecture. Until then, authors wrote science books for adults. Michael Faraday wrote this one for children, the first science book written especially for young people.

Service to his congregation and to Jesus remained a central part of his activities throughout his life. His Bible became well-used from his reading it and marking favorite passages. He seldom missed services at the church he and his wife attended. As an elder of the congregation, he also prepared and gave some of the sermons.

Michael Faraday died in 1867. He could have been buried in Westminster Abbey near the grave of Isaac Newton. Instead, he'd given instructions to be buried at the cemetery next to the church he had attended all of his life. His friends marked the grave with a headstone of the simplest sort, as he requested.

Whenever people list the top ten scientists of all time, they always include Michael Faraday. The greatest monuments to his name are the modern electrical devices around us every day.

6

A FORGOTTEN HERO

Joseph Henry is America's forgotten scientific hero. Although the public is hardly aware of his name, his discoveries are well known among scientists. He was both a great scientist and successful inventor. He is considered America's greatest electrical experimenter between the time of Benjamin Franklin and Thomas Edison.

The life of Joseph Henry followed a course like that of Michael Faraday. Both grew up in poverty. Both succeeded in getting an education through their own study and reading books. Both became great scientists but remained humble Christians.

At first, it looked as if Joseph Henry would not amount to much. As a child, he was expected to work to help support the family. He had a difficult time holding a job. No one could put a finger on the reason. He always seemed to be out of step with everyone else. One person said of Joseph Henry, "He isn't quite right in the head."

Joseph Henry also had a problem making up his mind. Once, his mother sent him to a shoe cobbler for a new pair of boots.

The cobbler began on Joseph's new boots. "Do you want square toes or round toes?" the cobbler asked.

Joseph Henry couldn't decide. He went for a walk trying to make up his mind. He delayed so long the cobbler had given up waiting for an answer. When Henry returned, the cobbler had made one boot with square toes and the other with round toes.

His mother earned extra income by taking in boarders. A boarder pays for a room and regular meals. One of the people staying in the Henry home had a book about science experiments. Joseph Henry chanced upon the book and began reading it. When the boarder saw Joseph Henry's interest in the subject, he gave the boy the book.

The book was so interesting Joseph Henry wanted to become a scientist. He tried to enroll at Albany Academy, a local college. The president pointed out that Joseph had not gone to high school. Joseph Henry began working through the high school textbooks. The president of the college helped him. He finished the entire high school course of study in only seven months.

He earned college tuition by teaching at a country school. After graduation, he became a teacher of science at the college.

He experimented with electricity and made a number of discoveries and inventions. He built electric motors, generators, and transformers. He did not publish reports of his discoveries. He assumed they were ideas already well known to scientists. Joseph Henry was first with these discoveries. In many cases, Michael Faraday made the same devices after Henry. Faraday received credit for the achievement because he published first.

In 1825, William Sturgeon, an English scientist, invented an electromagnet. He wrapped bare copper wire around a bar of iron. The bar was not magnetic. The instant current flowed through the wire the iron became magnetic. The instant he turned off the electricity, the iron lost its magnetism.

Sturgeon's electromagnet was only a toy. Joseph Henry studied the electromagnet with the goal of improving it. He quickly found he could make it stronger in two ways. He could increase the current, or he could wrap more turns of wire around the iron bar.

When he used too many coils of wire, the loops touched

one another and short-circuited. He insulated the wire by wrapping it with silk ribbon. With 800 turns of wire an ordinary battery could lift 27 pounds.

Henry learned to insulate the wires by painting them with shellac. Soon his electromagnets could lift a ton. He built the first commercial electromagnet. It extracted iron from crushed iron ore.

Joseph Henry demonstrated his discoveries at the College of New Jersey. He so impressed college officials they asked him to move there to teach. He agreed. A hundred years later Albert Einstein came to the same institution. By then it was world famous, and had changed its name to Princeton University.

Joseph Henry made small electromagnets, too, and put them to amusing uses. He built one that would ring a bell. With it, he invented the first electric doorbell. Students helped him string wires from his college laboratory to his home. Each day when he finished at his laboratory, he would press a button to ring the bell at home. When he arrived home his wife would have a cup of hot tea waiting for him. The distance from laboratory to home was one mile. He came very close to making the first telegraph.

An electric signal weakens as it flows through a long length of wire. Joseph Henry put little electromagnets in the circuit at regular intervals. Just before the current became too weak, the current would engage the magnets. They would kick in the next circuit connected to the next set of batteries. Henry's electric relay became an essential part of Samuel F.B. Morse's telegraph.

Samuel F. B. Morse came to Joseph Henry for help with the telegraph. Morse was a portrait painter. What he knew of electricity he'd learned by trial and error methods. During a one-week-long meeting, Joseph Henry explained the science behind electricity. The amount of help that Henry gave Morse is unknown because Henry agreed to keep secret what they discussed. However, before the meeting Morse had experienced a series of setbacks. Work on a telegraph line from Washington to Baltimore had come to a stop. After the meeting, Morse succeeded in completing the line from Washington to Baltimore. In 1836, Joseph Henry visited England. Faraday, Sturgeon, and other scientists gave him a warm welcome. He and Faraday became instant friends. They had much in common, including their Christian faith and humble nature. Neither Faraday nor Henry patented their inventions. They wanted the benefit of science to be available to as many people as possible.

Unknown to Joseph Henry, the United States Congress faced an unusual problem. Years earlier, James Smithson, a wealthy English scientist, had died and left his entire estate to the U.S. government. Smithson's will declared that Congress had to use the money for the "increase and diffusion of knowledge." Congress couldn't decide how to use the money. They solved their problem by appointing a board of regents to deal with the matter. The board couldn't decide what to do either. They established the Smithsonian Institution and selected America's best-known scientist — Joseph Henry — to run it.

Joseph Henry spent the money wisely. He began an ambitious plan to print books of recent scientific discoveries. He outfitted expeditions to explore the West, including the Grand Canyon. He used the telegraph to collect weather information and produced the first charts showing atmospheric conditions. His work led to the creation of the U.S. Weather Service.

Joseph Henry saw the approaching Civil War. He secretly bought medical supplies. He hid them in the Smithsonian building in Washington, D.C. The war lasted longer than anyone imagined it would. Joseph Henry's foresight saved hundreds of lives.

During the dark days of the war, Abraham Lincoln would invite Joseph Henry to the White House. They would discuss scientific matters and take the president's troubled mind off the war.

Late one night when the president couldn't sleep, he walked to the Smithsonian. Lincoln helped Joseph Henry with experiments with signal lanterns. A passerby noticed the late night signals. The next morning he turned in Joseph Henry as a southern spy. President Lincoln set the record straight.

After the Civil War Joseph Henry could have retired. However, he continued to direct the Smithsonian. In 1878, while Henry worked in his office, a young inventor came to visit him. The man, poorly dressed, was a teacher of speech. He had a crude electrical contraption for Joseph's inspection. The device used a small electromagnet in an attempt to turn human speech into an electrical signal.

Joseph Henry worked with the young man for several hours. He assured the inventor that he had a good idea. "My advice to you is that you work with it until you succeed."

The young inventor was Alexander Graham Bell. He took Joseph Henry's advice.

Alexander Graham Bell had been born in Edinburgh, Scotland, in 1847. His grandfather had studied the human voice. Vocal cords in the larynx vibrate rapidly to produce human speech. Musical instruments make sounds by vibrating reeds, strings, or tight membranes. All of these ways involve rapid back and forth motions. Air molecules are alternately compressed together and then released.

In Scotland, Alexander Graham Bell assisted his father in teaching deaf children. His father had developed a system of visible speech, a method of lip-reading.

The family moved from Edinburgh to Canada in 1870. Three years later Alexander became a professor at Boston University. He studied the physical causes of deafness. He fell in love with one of his deaf students, Mabel Hubbard. He was too poor to marry. This gave him an added reason to learn all he could about the science of sound.

As he studied and experimented, Alexander became convinced he could convert sound to electrical impulses. A wire could carry these impulses over great distances. He could then convert the electrical signals back into sound. He and an assistant named Thomas A. Watson worked to build such a device.

On March 10, 1876, Bell spilled some battery acid on himself. He said, "Mr. Watson, please come here. I want you." Watson had been in an upstairs room. He came down in great excitement. He heard Bell's voice perfectly from the telephone. In Bell's design, sound waves struck a thin iron diaphragm and caused it to vibrate. The vibrations affected a magnetic field of a nearby magnet. The changing magnetic field in turn caused variations in an electric current that passed through the field. The receiver at the other end reversed the process. The varying electric field caused an electromagnet to alternately attract and release a thin iron disk. This vibration caused sound waves.

Later, he changed the design. As before, when sound waves struck the mouthpiece, a thin metal disk vibrated back and forth. Now the disk compressed and released carbon particles. Carbon conducts electric current. An electric current flowing through the carbon grew stronger or weaker in perfect step to the sound waves. At the other end, an electromagnet pulled on a thin metal disk. The disk vibrated to generate sound waves.

After meeting with Joseph Henry, Alexander Graham Bell spent another year working on the telephone. In February 1876, Bell patented the telephone. He hurried to complete an improved model to demonstrate at the 1876 Centennial Exposition in Philadelphia. The fair celebrated the one hundredth anniversary of the Declaration of Independence.

The fair offered a series of awards, including one for the best invention. Unfortunately, Alexander Graham Bell missed the competition deadline for his telephone. He almost missed the show itself. Organizers made room for him behind some stairs.

Joseph Henry was one of the judges of the competition. Now Henry steered the committee around to see the telephone work. The extra attention made the telephone the hit of the exposition. Its simplicity amazed scientists who examined it. Joseph Henry was one of the judges. He took the extra effort to see that the telephone received a special award.

With the success of his invention, Alexander Graham Bell

could at last afford to marry. Mabel encouraged him to sell the invention. Bell offered it to the Western Union Telegraph Company. He asked $100,000. They turned him down. They could see no particular use for a machine that talks.

Bell's friends urged him to start his own company. They offered to invest in his invention. The new company, The Bell Telephone Company, was incredibly successful. It changed its name to American Telephone and Telegraph. As AT&T it became the largest private company in the world.

With his success, Bell could now do whatever he wanted. What he wanted to do did not change. Before he became wealthy

On October 18, 1892, Alexander Graham Bell first used the telephone line connecting New York and Chicago.

he had helped the deaf and perfected new inventions. Now as a millionaire he could do it on a much grander scale.

Bell built a summer home in Nova Scotia, Canada. There he experimented with heavy lift kites and early flying machines. He built a research hanger for Glenn H. Curtiss, an aviation pioneer. Together they designed planes that could take off and land on water. They made improvements to the Wright brothers' airplane. It was Curtiss, and not the Wrights, who made the first public, mile-long flight of an airplane in the United States.

Some of Bell's other inventions include the metal detector and the iron lung. The iron lung kept alive a person who couldn't breathe because of injury or illness.

Bell continued to press for improved telephone service. In 1915 his company had lines that crossed the country. Bell took part in a ceremony to place the first telephone call across the United States. He was on the East Coast. His assistant Watson was on the West Coast. Bell said, "Watson, please come here. I want you."

Bell continued to teach deaf students. One of his most famous students was Helen Keller, who was both blind and deaf. She wrote a book about her life and dedicated it to Alexander Graham Bell.

Both Samuel F.B. Morse and Alexander Graham Bell owe some measure of their success to Joseph Henry. However, Henry never claimed credit for his role in making the telegraph or telephone possible and he never patented any of his inventions. One of his discoveries was that whenever electricity first flows in a circuit, it causes a force that resists the flow. The unit in the metric system for measuring this force is named the henry in his honor.

Joseph Henry was noted as a dedicated Christian who spoke to God in prayer whenever he had to make an important decision. He included prayer as part of his laboratory routine.

7

MESSAGES ACROSS
THE ATLANTIC

For such a small country, Scotland has a large number of people who became world famous. James Boswell is famous for his biography of Samuel Johnson. Arthur Conan Doyle created the character of Sherlock Holmes. Robert Louis Stevenson wrote *Treasure Island* and other famous works. Sir Walter Scott wrote *Ivanhoe* and the Waverly novels. Robert Burns was a world-famous poet. All these writers were from Scotland.

Missionaries from Scotland include David Livingstone, who explored Africa, and Mary Slessor, another missionary to Africa. James I, the son of Mary, Queen of Scots, became the king of England. He authorized a new translation of the Bible, the King James translation.

Scottish inventors include John Dunlop who made the modern air-inflated tire. James Watt perfected the steam engine. James Young found that petroleum could replace whale oil as a fuel. James Dewar invented the vacuum bottle. Alexander Graham Bell, who invented the telephone, was born in Scotland and educated at Edinburgh.

Medical researchers include Alexander Fleming who discovered penicillin and James Simpson who pioneered the use of painkillers in operations.

One of the great scientists from Scotland was William Thomson. His mother died when he was six years old and his father raised him. In 1832 his father became a physics professor at Glasgow University in Scotland. William showed an early interest in science. He began classes at the university at age 10 years. By the time he was 22 years old, William Thomson had become a college professor. He'd studied at Glasgow, graduated from Cambridge, went to Paris for advanced study, and then back to Glasgow to teach science. He was one of the first scientists to follow his lectures with experiments in the laboratory.

One of the first subjects he investigated was heat. A debate raged among scientists about the nature of heat.

What is heat? Until the 1800s, most scientists believed heat to be a substance. Heat did seem to flow. Suppose a warm object touches a cold object. The warm object will grow cooler while the cold object will grow warmer. Scientists reasoned that heat must be a substance. It flows from a body with too much heat into another body with too little heat.

If heat were a substance, then why couldn't scientists weigh it? Scientists weighed a metal ball. Then they heated the ball white-hot and weighed it again. Because it had gained the heat substance, the ball should have weighed more. It didn't. Whether cold or hot, an object weighed the same.

About 50 years earlier, Count Rumford had made a discovery that puzzled scientists. Count Rumford was an American-born scientist who lived in Europe. In 1798 he supervised the boring of cannons out of blocks of brass. The drilling caused both the drill and the cannon to get hot. He had to continuously pour water over the drill and cannon to cool them. An endless supply of heat seemed to come out of the brass.

Count Rumford concluded that heat is a form of energy. He believed that the mechanical energy of the drill changed into heat.

Many scientists agreed with Count Rumford. They sought a way to figure out how much heat a given amount of mechanical energy could produce. They called this the mechanical equivalent of heat. How much mechanical work must you do to produce a given amount of heat? No one succeeded in finding how to calculate this quantity.

In 1847, William Thomson read a report by James Joule, an amateur scientist with a fascination for measuring changes in temperatures. On his honeymoon, James Joule would stop the carriage at waterfalls. He measured the temperature of the water at the top of the waterfall and again at the bottom of the falls. The water was warmer at the bottom than at the top. The energy of the falling water changed into heat energy.

Joule made thermometers that could read changes in temperatures of tiny fractions of degrees. A person could come into a closed room, sit quietly for a moment and leave. His thermometer could measure the change in room temperature from the person's body heat.

In one experiment, Joule measured the mechanical energy that went into turning a crank that he attached to paddles. The paddles churned water. He compared the heat gained by the water with the mechanical energy that went into turning the crank. From this experiment, he calculated the mechanical equivalent of heat.

James Joule was self taught. He had no academic standing. He sent his report to the Royal Society. They turned it down. He sent it to scientific journals. They ignored it. Finally, he gave a public lecture at Manchester, England. Scientists stayed away. James had a friend on the Manchester newspaper. The friend published the text of the speech.

The newspaper report came to the attention of William Thomson. He decided to attend James Joule's next lecture. At the end of the talk, only one of the professors asked questions — William Thomson. Although only 23 years old, William Thomson was well known and respected. Because he took an interest in James Joule's lecture, the other professors did, too. In a short time, James Joule went from an obscure amateur scientist to a world famous authority on heat. Now the Royal

Society invited him to speak. In 1850, they elected him a member.

William Thomson and James Joule worked together in experiments that measured how a gas grows cooler as it expands. They were both Christians and got along well together.

They discovered the principle that if a gas is allowed to expand freely it will become cooler. This is the principle behind refrigerators and air conditioners. In the refrigerator a liquid is pumped through coils and allowed to change into a gas. As the gas expands, it cools the inside of the refrigerator. Then it is pumped outside where it is compressed and changed back into a liquid. The heat it picks up is released through cooling vanes at the back of the refrigerator.

Experiments by Thomson and Joule made it clear that heat is motion — the motion of atoms and molecules. In Count Rumford's experiment, the friction of the rotating drill was transferred to the atoms and molecules of the cannon. These atoms and molecules are in constant motion. When a substance gains heat, its atoms move more vigorously. When a substance grows cooler, its atoms move less quickly.

Atoms in solids cannot move as freely as in a gas. But they do move. They vibrate around a central location. When a hammer strikes a nail, the energy from the motion of the hammer is not lost. It goes into the nail and into the head of the hammer, causing their atoms to shake about violently. The head of the nail becomes warm.

When a substance cools, its atoms move more slowly.

William Thomson asked himself, "How cold must a substance be for its atoms to stop moving?"

Imagine a temperature so cold all motion ceased. This would be the absolutely coldest temperature possible. A body at this temperature cannot be cooled any further because its atoms have lost all motion.

William Thomson called this temperature absolute zero.

He recalled a discovery made by Jacques Charles, a French scientist. Jacques Charles recorded the volume of various gases as they expanded and contracted while being heated and cooled. When he cooled any gas by one degree Celsius, it lost a volume equal to 1/273 of its volume at zero degrees Celsius (32°F).

This was the clue that William Thomson needed. His calculations convinced him that -273°C was absolute zero — the coldest temperature possible. He suggested that scientists use a temperature scale that began at this temperature.

Scientists found many advantages in measuring temperatures from absolute zero. In later life, William Thomson received the title of Baron Kelvin. He became well known under that name. Scientists named the absolute temperature scale in his honor — the Kelvin scale. The freezing point of water is

*William
Thomson*

273 degrees Kelvin (273°K). Room temperature is about 291°K. While studying heat, Thomson developed one of the most important laws in all of science. He realized that whenever energy changes from one form to another, some heat is generated. Heat energy is the random motion of atoms and molecules. The study of the flow of heat is known as thermodynamics, "thermo" means heat and "dynamics" means motion. Thomson stated the second law of thermodynamics: the universe as a whole is becoming more disorganized as other forms of energy change into the random motion of heat energy.

This discovery was one of Thomson's key arguments against evolution. According to the second law of thermodynamics, the universe left to itself becomes more disorganized. However, evolution requires that the universe become more organized. He believed that science showed that God had created the earth and its life.

Along with heat, electricity interested William Thomson. While in college, he had helped his instructor build batteries to demonstrate electricity to the rest of the class.

Shortly before the American Civil War, Cyrus Field (American businessman, 1819–1892) began the daunting task of laying an Atlantic telegraph cable. He spent his own personal fortune and years of his life on the project. If it worked, messages could be quickly flashed between New York City and London. Messages would cross 4,000 miles of wire under the Atlantic Ocean.

The first four cables broke. The fifth was completed on August 5, 1858. But the line had problems. An operator would key a single crisp dot at one end. At the other end, the short pulse of electricity came out as a long and weak signal. Dots and dashes overran one another. Field's engineers believed a powerful electric current would solve the problem. They punched each message through the telegraph with a powerful surge of electrical energy. The signal grew weaker day by day. After two months the line failed.

After the Civil War, Cyrus Field tried again. This time he

used the monster ship *Great Eastern*. It was five times bigger than any other vessel then afloat. Cyrus Field tore out the luxurious cabins to make room for the cable. The huge size of the ship made it steadier and paying out the cable was easier. Despite the crew's best efforts, the cable snapped and the crew could not recover the broken end.

A year later Cyrus Field was ready to try again. This time he asked William Thomson to be the chief scientist in charge of the trans-Atlantic telegraph. William Thomson suggested powering the telegraph with the barest trickle of current. Critics of Thomson asked how he would detect such a weak current. William Thomson invented sensitive receivers to detect faint electric signals.

One of his devices used a tiny electromagnet powered by the faint signals. As electricity from the faraway dots and dashes arrived, they caused the electromagnet to turn a tiny metal rod. Attached to the rod was a mirror. A beam of light struck the mirror. The mirror had to wiggle only a little and it would reflect the beam a great amount. The light beam danced to the signals of dots and dashes coming from New York.

In the 1800s, many people believed bigger and more powerful was better. William Thomson proved that this was not always the case. Small, delicate, and sensitive electrical instruments succeeded where powerful electrical devices failed. His delicate little instruments were years ahead of their time.

With the success of the trans-Atlantic cable, others were laid, including one across the much broader Pacific Ocean. William Thomson held the patents on the telegraph receivers. He became wealthy and bought a private yacht, the 126-ton *Lalla Rookh*. He enjoyed traveling, and combined his interest in scientific invention with his ocean voyages. He invented an improved compass and the first computer for predicting tides.

Queen Victoria knighted William Thomson for his efforts in making the trans-Atlantic telegraph successful. Later, he served as president of the Royal Society. When he died in 1907, he was buried in Westminster Abbey.

William Thomson, like so many of the great people from Scotland, was a devout Christian. He believed in the Bible and held it up as the most important book in his life. He encouraged religious instruction from the Bible in British schools.

8

LIGHTS, CAMERA, ACTION

On any list of the world's greatest inventors, Thomas Alva Edison is usually at the top. Edison was born in Milan, Ohio, on February 11, 1847. He received only three months of education in a public school. His teachers told his mother that he was "addled," a term that meant his mind was not right. His mother knew Edison could read almost as fast as he could turn pages and could remember practically everything he read. She took him out of the school and educated him at home.

At age 12, he began selling newspapers aboard a train as it made its run to Detroit. Later, he bought secondhand printing equipment and published his own paper to sell to train passengers. One day, Edison rescued a small boy who had strayed onto the train tracks. As a reward, his grateful father offered to teach Edison to be a telegraph operator. Within a year, Edison became the best and fastest operator in the United States. With the money he earned he bought books about electricity written by Michael Faraday.

In 1863, Edison became a telegraph operator for the railroad. He was 16 years old. He began to experiment with electrical devices. In 1869, he had his first important invention, the stock ticker. He modified a telegraph so it printed on a strip of paper. The paper continuously displayed the price of stock being traded on stock exchanges. He sold the stock ticker for $40,000, an incredible sum. The payment was not due to hard bargaining on his part. He had been prepared to give it up for $500 but did not have the courage to ask for so much. Instead, the buyer suggested $40,000.

With the money, Edison built his own research laboratory at Menlo Park, New Jersey. So many important devices came from his laboratory that he became known as the wizard of Menlo Park. In all, he turned out 1,300 inventions. Some of his inventions were as simple as waxed paper. Others included the phonograph, electric light, and motion picture projector.

In 1877, Edison demonstrated the phonograph. The word phonograph is from a Greek word *phono* meaning sound or speech and *graph* meaning to write. A phonograph is a sound writer. Edison's first model had a needle that touched tinfoil wrapped around a cylinder. One spoke into a funnel-shaped megaphone. The sound waves caused the needle to vibrate in time with the sound waves. While the person spoke, a crank caused the cylinder to rotate. The needle skimmed over the tinfoil and left wavy grooves on the cylinder that exactly matched the sound waves. Edison recited "Mary Had a Little Lamb." The cylinder containing the child's rhyme still exists today.

As soon as the phonograph was working, Edison turned to the problem of electric light. Until then, people lighted their homes with candles, kerosene or whale oil lamps, or gaslight. Burning acetylene gas produced a brilliant light, as did a powerful arc of electricity between carbon terminals. Both were far too brilliant and dangerous for daily use in a home. All of these light sources had the risk of explosion or fire.

Until the 1800s, the activity of people at night was greatly hindered by the lack of dependable light. Only a few cities had streetlights. Most homes in the city had guestrooms. If a visitor came over but stayed until after dark, it was polite to offer the visitor lodging for the night because it was not safe to walk unlighted city streets at night. Safe, dependable lighting would change all of that. Factories could work around the clock. Streets would become safer. Even baseball games could be played at night. Although others made electric light bulbs, including Joseph Sawn in England, Edison's version proved to be more reliable.

In 1879, Edison's first carbon filament light bulb burned for 40 hours. Within a year, he made bulbs that glowed for 1,500 hours and he began marketing them. The first commercial bulb was 16 watts. The filament was of carbon made from a scorched cotton thread.

Thomas Edison with his improved phonograph.

Edison made the first practical motion picture equipment. The early motion pictures had short scenes. Only one or two people at a time could view the flickering scene. Edison printed the images on a transparent film. A strong light shined through the film and projected the images on a screen. An auditorium full of people could see the same movie. Edison also invented a camera with the ability to continuously record images. He filmed the first motion picture that told a story, *The Great Train Robbery*. The first pictures were silent movies. One of the problems that inventors faced in making talking movies was a way to amplify sound.

Edison could not hear well, and his deafness grew worse with time. Like so many great people, he looked on the bright side. He pointed out that his deafness saved him from distractions.

However, inventors realized that some way to amplify sound would be necessary for inventions such as the phonograph, radio, and motion pictures to play to a large audience.

Thomas Edison himself had made a discovery that would help amplify electric signals, although he was not aware of its importance. In one of his experiments to improve the electric light bulb, he sealed an unheated wire near the glowing filament of the light bulb. The unheated wire was not connected to an electric current. When he tested the unheated wire, he was surprised to see that a small current flowed. Further tests showed that electrons boiled off the hot filament and jumped across the gap to the cool wire. Edison saw no particular use for this observation. He wrote about it in his notebooks, patented the discovery, and described it in a technical journal so others could benefit from his discovery.

Edison's report came to the attention of John Ambrose Fleming, an English electrical engineer. Fleming served as a consultant for Edison's company in London, England. Later, he worked with Guglielmo Marconi in perfecting the wireless telegraph. Marconi's wireless telegraph sent Morse code dot and dash messages through the air without wires. It was the

*Guglielmo Marconi (1874–1937), an Italian, developed
the wireless radio. Here he is shown operating the
radio on a ship at sea.*

first kind of radio. To test his invention, Marconi set up his
receiver in St. Johns, Newfoundland, on the North American
continent. Fleming was at the transmitter in Cornwall, England,
on the other side of the Atlantic. Fleming keyed in the Morse
code for the letter S that became the first wireless signal trans-
mitted across the Atlantic Ocean.

Fleming became a professor of electrical engineering at a
college in London. He investigated Thomas Edison's discovery that electrons boil away from a hot filament connected to a
source of electricity. Normally, the electrons stay near the hot
filament. Fleming drew them away by putting a small metal
plate with a positive charge nearby. The positive plate attracted

the negative electrons. The electrons flowed from the hot filament to the cool plate.

Fleming called his device a valve. It is known today as a diode, from the letters "di" meaning two, and "ode" from electrode. A diode has two electrodes. Fleming's diode detected radio waves and converted them to weak direct current that could be played through a radio headset.

During the early 1900s, the idea of using radio to broadcast music and news seemed wildly fanciful. Yet, on Christmas Eve 1906, astonished wireless operators at sea on the Atlantic heard music instead of dots and dashes in their headsets. The music came from an experimental radio station near Boston, Massachusetts. The first broadcast was a violin solo playing the song "O Holy Night," followed by a Bible reading.

It is interesting to note that so many inventions are closely associated with the Bible. The first book Gutenberg printed was the Bible. The first message sent by the telegraph, "What hath God wrought," was a quotation from the Bible. The first radio broadcast was a Christian hymn and a Bible reading.

A simple modification of the diode by American inventor Lee De Forest changed it into an amplifying triode. The diode and triode were known as vacuum tubes. The electrodes were in a glass tube in which the air had been pumped out. Vacuum tubes working one after another made weak electric signals thousands of times stronger. John Ambrose Fleming lived to see vacuum tubes such as his diode and Lee De Forest's triode become the key invention of the electronic age during the first half of the 1900s. Even today, vacuum tubes have not been entirely replaced by semiconductors. Vacuum tubes are found in microwave ovens and in devices that must withstand high heat and carry strong electric current.

John Ambrose Fleming died in 1945 at the age of 95. Fleming's long life was filled with honors for his contributions to electronics, radio, and television. In addition, he was an active Christian and wrote a major book defending the account of creation in the Bible.

9

THE FIRST COMPUTER

C harles Babbage was the son of a wealthy English banker. Science, especially mathematics, fascinated the young Babbage. He was largely self-taught in that subject. He attended Cambridge University in England in 1810. It saddened him to see the poor state of mathematical instruction at the university. The professors were far behind the rest of the world.

While at Cambridge, Charles Babbage heard about a remarkable invention. The Frenchman Joseph Marie Jacquard invented a way to mechanically control a loom that weaves cloth. Colored thread made the pattern in a fabric. As the loom operated, hooks rose and caught the thread to draw it down into the fabric being woven. Jacquard found that he could control the hooks by holes that he punched in cards. Where there was a hole the hook could rise and catch its thread. The absence of a hole prevented the hook from catching the thread.

Jacquard's placed his cards of heavy cardboard end to end. He connected them by twine. They moved forward like a conveyor belt. The cards held the pattern for the fabric. When a loom operator finished a particular bolt of fabric, he could set the cards aside. He replaced them with a different set of cards to give an entirely different pattern to the next bolt.

The Jacquard loom was exceptionally successful. The cards programmed the loom to produce fabric with intricate patterns.

France soon had 12,000 looms controlled by punched cards in operation.

Charles Babbage believed that someone in England should have invented the card-controlled loom. "England is falling behind the rest of the world," he concluded

"No," the members of the Royal Society said. "We have the discoveries of the great Isaac Newton."

Even their respect of Isaac Newton hindered progress. Isaac Newton had invented calculus, a powerful form of mathematics. His notations — the symbols he used — were clumsy and could be confused with one another. Calculations using his notation were prone to error. Mathematicians in Europe used a different notation. These symbols were simpler and easier to use. British mathematicians ignored the improved system in favor of the older one.

Charles Babbage said, "Isaac Newton died a hundred years ago. England is living in the past. We need to take a lead in trying out new ideas. We should train new scientists and reward those who are successful."

Slowly, England heeded Charles Babbage's call to action. England decided to begin a regular mail service, the first in the world. The Postal Commission asked Charles Babbage how best to charge for delivering the mail. They asked, "Should we charge by the weight or by the distance the letter travels or both?"

Charles did a time and motion study. He measured how long it took a postal employee to weigh a letter, locate its destination on a map, figure the mileage, and then calculate the charge. The cost of mailing a letter would be quite high.

A few years earlier, an English schoolteacher, Rowland Hill, had proposed the use of prepaid stamps at a flat fee, regardless of distance. Charles Babbage tested this idea. What if the postal service charged the same amount for carrying a letter, regardless of the distance? Assume the letter weighed a half-ounce or less. Most letters of one or two pages would be under that weight. All letters could go for flat fee.

This seemed to go against common sense. Why should a person mailing a letter across town pay as much as a person sending a letter across the country? Charles Babbage pointed to his figures. The flat rate would be so inexpensive it would not matter. The British government adopted his recommendation. A letter could go anywhere in the country for a one-penny stamp. The British postal service proved especially successful. People liked the new system. They

Charles Babbage, a 19th century English inventor, designed his difference engine to calculate and print multiplication tables. It failed because parts could not be manufactured.

could buy stamps and use them as needed. They did not have to stand in line and wait for a post office clerk to figure the charge for each letter.

Postal authorities from other countries came to England to learn how it worked. They adopted Britain's system. This time Britain had led the world.

Besides being a mathematician, Charles Babbage was an inventor. He invented the speedometer and several other useful devices including an instrument for examining the inside of the eye. For most of his life, he worked on designing and building a multi-purpose calculating machine.

Mathematicians grew weary of long and complicated calculations. For that reason they calculated common quantities and saved them in published books as look-up tables. Unfortunately, now and then they would find that one of the tables had an error. A calculating machine would make it possible to check the tables for errors. Maybe the calculating machine could replace the need for mathematical tables.

Charles Babbage was not the first person with an interest in calculating machines. In the early 1600s, German astronomer Johannes Kepler had built one as had French scientist Blaise Pascal. Both machines used a series of wheels that connected with one another. Each wheel had gears with ten teeth. A full turn of one wheel would engage the next wheel and rotate its gear by one notch. Ten turns caused the next wheel to rotate once. Ten turns of the second wheel advanced the third wheel by one turn, and so on. The wheels counted by 1, 10, 100, and so on. Pascal's machine could add and subtract.

A few years later Gottfried Leibnitz, a German mathematician, added to the design so it could do multiplication and division. Both machines were slow and could be used only for the simplest calculations. Almost two hundred years passed with only slight improvements to the designs.

Charles Babbage's idea went far beyond what anyone else had ever imagined. He started in the 1830s on a design for what he called an analytical engine. It would be as large as a railroad locomotive and as intricate as a watch. Its physical innards were a complicated array of rods, cylinders, and racks upon racks of gears. Bells announced progress toward an answer. A printer gave the final result.

It also read punched cards similar to those for the Jacquard loom. The cards input the numbers used in the calculation. The machine stored partial answers on punched cards. It could act on the cards later.

Punched cards also contained instructions to tell the machine what calculations to make with the numbers. In other words, Charles Babbage could program his machine.

One person who encouraged Charles Babbage to finish his machine was Ada Augusta, the Countess of Lovelace. Her father was Lord Byron, the famous English poet. She was one

Babbage's multiplier: The computing element of Babbage's elaborate machine for multiplying was a series of toothed wheels on shafts. they worked like the wheels of a modern mileage indicator.

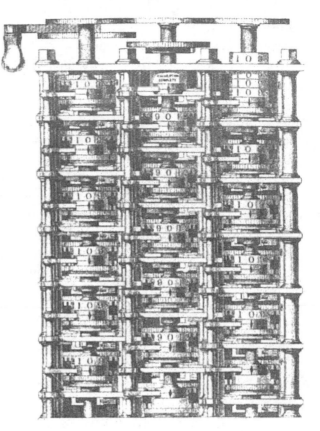

of the few people who recognized the importance of Babbage's work. Her enthusiasm matched his. She explained, "The analytical engine weaves algebraic patterns, just as the Jacquard loom weaves flowers and leaves."

Ada became the first person to write a program for a computer. Once a program for a particular calculation was entered on punched cards, the cards could be stacked with a different program to perform that particular operation. She believed the machine could do far more than calculate numbers. It might compose music, she said, or generate graphics and other unimagined practical uses.

Charles Babbage's analytical engine was a grand design.

Unfortunately, it remained just that — a design. Despite 50 years of work, despite an immense sum of money being spent, Charles Babbage never finished the analytical engine. The technology of his day simply could not support the intricate precision of his design. Part of the amazing machine still exists. Visitors to London can see it in the Science Museum.

Charles Babbage died in 1871. Many people looked upon him as an eccentric failure. Sixty years passed. In 1937, Howard H. Aiken, a student at Harvard University, came across Babbage's description of the analytical engine. He caught the enthusiasm Babbage had for creating a calculating machine.

Technology had improved enough to do it. Aiken, working with IBM, constructed Mark I, the first general-purpose calculating machine. An electronic computer replaced it a few years later. Charles Babbage had been a hundred years ahead of his time.

Did Charles Babbage consider himself a failure? No, because the analytical engine was not of prime importance in his life. His most important goal was to be true to his Christian faith. While a student at Cambridge, Charles Babbage met with others who were Christians. They resolved to dedicate their lives to God. They agreed to strive to leave the world a better place than they had found it.

Near the end of his life, Charles Babbage did not appear unduly troubled that his great engine would be incomplete. It was as if he could see into the future to a time when calculating machines were common place. He could see that his life had made a difference.